The ROAD MAP

to

Greatness

Published and printed by Ignite Publishing™ a division of JBO Global Inc.
5569-47th Street Red Deer, AB
Canada, T4N1S1 1-877-677-6115

Editor-in-Chief JB Owen
Typesetting by Kristine Joy Magno & graphics work by Sinisa Poznanovic

Edited by JB Owen, Mimi Safiyah, Zoe Wong, and Steph Elliott
Designed in Canada
Printed in China
ISBN: 979-8-9910888-0-0

Ordering Information: Quantity sales. Special discounts are available on quantity purchases by corporations, associations, and others. For details, contact the publisher at the above address. Programs, products, or services provided by the authors are found by contacting them directly.

Testimonials

You have been pivotal in MY story JB. And so today, I honor the remarkable woman you are, knighted for your humanitarian work and an unstoppable force of nature. I thank you for your furnace of faith and your effervescent fun, your kilometers of courage and above all for your vision to really leave a legacy. You have ignited millions of people around the world with stories of hope and healing. You are building schools of empowerment all over the world. But you have changed this one life, more than you will ever know.

Alison Weihe

I am genuinely grateful for the opportunity to work with such a dedicated team committed to a profound mission. I extend my heartfelt gratitude to Lady JB Owen for providing this platform that unites us through our stories and kindles the greatness within each of us.

Farrah Smith

JB is more then just touching lives, she is changing lives. She has offered sound and creative input in providing advice around business and life. I am thrilled to work with her again on the next big step of my journey. I appreciate her intergrity and passion in helping me build my own legacy.

Andonia Reynolds

She not only has the power of the pen, but she knows how to gift that power to others. She has changed my life, as well as so many other's lives. That has allowed all of us to change lives by our written and spoken words. What a positive impact on the world!

Melanie Summers

The training, development, and support that I have experienced have been at an even higher standard than I expected. She has given me the tools to learn and grow in my life and business. You will not be disappointed working with her!

Cheryl Rafter

Lady JB offers us a connection to something bigger than ourselves, which somehow makes previously daunting and out-of-reach pipedreams become not only possible but utterly doable.

Tracy Stone

Lady JB is the most generous person I know. This opportunity is truly incredible!

Nicole Shantel Freeman

This experience was exciting and freeing. Thank you, for giving me a platform to help inspire others!

Aly Incardona

The journey with Lady JB Owen is inspiring and motivating toward a better world.

Ash Bhadani

Dedication

I dedicate this book to my Uncle George and my Auntie Sharon. They are the first *real* people I saw being great in their lives, great in their business, great in their aspirations, and greatly achieving success. I also saw them being great to one another, great to their kids, family, and the people who worked for them. Most importantly they were great to me, showing unconditional love and everlasting interest in the greatness I was aspiring for. For as long as I can remember and to this very day they have always shown the most care and support for me finding my way and standing within the greatness that exists in me.

The Roadmap to Greatness

Bestselling books by Lady JB Owen

Letter For My Mother
Enjoying Parenting
30 Ways to Ignite Your Legacy in 30 Days
Wisdom From the Back of a Bike

Best-selling compilation books by IGNITE Featuring Lady JB Owen

Ignite Your Life for Women
Ignite Your Female Leadership
Ignite Your Parenting
Ignite Your Life for Men
Ignite Your Life for Conscious Leaders
Ignite Your Health and Wellness
Ignite Your Adventurous Spirit
Ignite Female Change Makers
Ignite the Modern Goddess
Ignite Happiness
Ignite Love
Ignite Your Inner Spirit
Ignite the Entrepreneur
Ignite Possibilities
Ignite the Hunger in You
Ignite Your Wisdom
Ignite Forgiveness
Ignite Faith
Ignite Your Purpose
Ignite Your Courage
Ignite Joy

" *There is nothing greater than the greatness that lies within* **"**

JB Owen

Introduction

Dear Reader,

Welcome to *The Roadmap to Greatness*. I am thrilled and honored to accompany you on this transformative journey toward unlocking the extraordinary potential within you. My name is Lady JB Owen, and through my work as a legacy mentor, speaker, publisher, and CEO of the Ignite brand, I have had the privilege of witnessing countless individuals *Ignite* their inner flame and achieve remarkable success.

Greatness is not reserved for a select few; it is within reach for each one of us. It lies in our ability to *dream boldly*, to *push past our limitations*, and to *rise after every fall*. Greatness is the courage to step into the unknown, the ability to persevere through challenges, and the passion to pursue what sets *our souls on fire.*

In my journey, I have learned that the path to greatness is not always a straight line. It is filled with twists and turns, highs and lows, and moments of doubt. Yet, it is precisely these experiences that shape us, strengthen us, and prepare us for the extraordinary. The key is to recognize that within each of us is a precious spark—a tiny flame of unlimited potential that, when nurtured and fueled, can illuminate our path and the paths of those around us to a *place of greatness.*

I have written this book to be your guide, your companion, and your inspiration. It is designed to help you awaken that spark, navigate the inevitable challenges, and ultimately uncover your inner greatness. You will find practical strategies, insightful stories, and powerful exercises to support you at every stage. Whether you are just beginning to explore your potential or are on your way to achieving your dreams, this 'roadmap' will provide you with the tools and encouragement you need to reach new heights.

As you discover your greatness, you will soon realize it is not just about personal achievement; it is about positively impacting yourself *and* others. It is about using your unique skills and talents to inspire, uplift, and empower those around you. As you embark on this journey, know your success is *not* for you alone. It is a beacon of hope and possibility for many other people. By igniting your innate greatness, you contribute to a collective improvement of positive change and transformation for all of humanity.

I encourage you to approach this journey with an open heart and an open mind. Embrace the process, celebrate your progress, and be kind to yourself along the way. Trust in the power of your inner compass and let it guide you toward a life of *purpose, fulfillment,* and the *greatest enjoyment* possible.

Thank you for allowing me to be your guide. Together, we will Ignite the extraordinary greatness within you and create a brighter, more collective world.

With heartfelt gratitude and anticipation,
Lady JB Owen

Chapter 1

Awakening the Flame Within

The Spark of True Potential

In the quiet moments of our lives, a tiny spark of potential often lies dormant within us, waiting to be ignited. That spark is the essence of our greatness, the seed from which our true potential can grow. For many, that spark remains unacknowledged, overshadowed by doubt, fear, or the mundane routines of daily life. However, recognizing and nurturing that spark is the first step on the road to finding one's greatness from within.

I believe that everyone possesses that inner flame and is capable of extraordinary brilliance. My journey began with a single realization that *the power to change my life lies within me.* That realization was the beginning of a voyage and the path that took me toward finding my inner greatness. It was a hard and tumultuous journey, yet it was filled with joy and magnificence. I had two choices: avoid the perils and difficulties that came with searching for my greatness and never experience the delights that were embedded within the journey, or endure the lessons to reap the blessings and discover what greatness I possessed. I chose the latter, and it has shown me that if one seeks to find it, one's greatness will happily be revealed.

For many, the concept of greatness is often tied to tangible accomplishments. Athletes who break records, business leaders who amass fortunes, and artists who achieve widespread recognition are typically seen as the epitome of greatness. These achievements are certainly admirable and require immense talent, dedication, and hard work. However, focusing solely on these external markers can create a narrow and sometimes misleading definition of what it means to be truly great.

I prefer to see greatness as the uniqueness that we each possess. It is not about the achievements but the talents and gifts we each have that make us one of a kind and like no other. Greatness is not a measurement but an *embodiment* of who we are, bringing forth our individual strengths in ways that help, support, inspire, teach, console, and serve. By embracing and sharing our unique qualities, we contribute to the betterment of our community and society. This collectively strengthens our world, making it a richer, more compassionate place while reinforcing the idea that true greatness lies within our authenticity and the individualized impact we choose to make.

The Essence of True Greatness

True greatness transcends the external accolades and milestones we often covet to achieve. Instead, it is found in the values we uphold, the behaviors we exhibit, and the positive contributions we make to our families, communities, and society. Greatness is not merely about *what* we achieve but *how* we achieve it and the *impact we leave behind.*

The mark of true greatness extends far beyond 'personal' victories. Greatness influences and inspires those around us, creating the possibility of reaching new heights and inspiring similar actions in others. When we rise, others rise, and when we prioritize values and behaviors over mere achievements, we foster environments where others also want to thrive and succeed.

A more collective approach to greatness contributes to a more compassionate, resilient, and interconnected society. A place we all want to live because it supports and encourages greatness for everyone. This collective elevation propels us all toward a more empowered life. Recognizing that our greatness contributes to the *greater good* places us on the cusp of our fullest potential. It reminds us that our journey is not just about individual success but about being a beacon of possibility for others. By living authentically and fostering our inner greatness, we become catalysts for a more enlightened and connected world.

The Collective Power of Greatness

When we begin to realize that our greatness is part of a larger collective, we unlock a profound truth: our individual contributions are vital threads in the fabric of a better humanity. By embracing this interconnectedness, we understand that our actions, values, and behaviors can uplift not only ourselves but also those we live and work with daily. Living in alignment with our true potential and fostering our greatness helps raise the consciousness of others, creating a ripple effect of positive change outward and beyond.

Greatness can be like a wildfire. *Once the flame is lit, it has the potential to spread rapidly, igniting a passion for excellence in someone else.* An initial spark of greatness, fueled by dedication and authenticity, becomes a beacon of inspiration. As others witness the transformative power of someone living in their greatness, they, too, are encouraged to tap into their own unique potential. This contagious energy creates a chain reaction, where each person's greatness fuels another's, resulting in a collective upgrade. The wildfire of greatness doesn't just elevate individuals; it strengthens communities, fostering innovation and propeling individuals toward greater aspirations. When we activate that inner flame, we become catalysts for widespread positive improvements, demonstrating that true greatness is both powerful and boundlessly influential.

As you discover your greatness, know it is more than just about you. Your journey to uncover and embrace your unique gifts has the power to uplift those around you. As you find and begin to use your greatness, you encourage others to do the same in their lives. Just like one candle has the capacity to light millions of other candles, your greatness can brighten the path for countless people in your home, your town, your country, and beyond. By sharing your light, you create an accumulated effect that fosters a community of empowered individuals, each contributing to the greater good of all humanity. You then become a catalyst for collective transformation, demonstrating that *true greatness lies in elevating others while elevating oneself.*

Chapter 2:

Values That Define Greatness

The Impact of True Greatness

Defining our greatness involves shifting our focus from external accomplishments to values and behaviors that define our character and contributions to the world. By embracing *empowering characteristics*, we elevate ourselves and motivate others to reevaluate their values and find ones that serve a greater purpose. True greatness is about making a positive difference in the lives of those around us by giving them an understanding that where they are is *not where they need to stay.* Too often, we remain stuck in our circumstances and conditioning. When we witness great will and determination, we soon find those same qualities within ourselves.

When I was striving to be better in my life, I decided to embark on a journey that was both grand and daunting. With a burning desire to inspire others, I rode 10,000 km across Canada on a tandem bike with my husband. That adventure spanned seventy-nine days, testing every fiber of my being. Through relentless rain, drizzling snow, towering mountains, endless roads, and encounters with threatening wildlife, I pushed through all my limiting beliefs, determined to uncover the greatness I had within me.

One day, while climbing a mountain in a blinding rainstorm, the fog was so thick that we could only see ten to twelve feet ahead. We were pelted by sheets of water from the passing traffic. It was a perilous trek, with the risk of being hit by a vehicle, going over the side rails, or our tires losing their grip on the wet road and wiping out. In that moment of physical and emotional challenge, I discovered my innate greatness. It wasn't the treacherous mountain climb or the harsh weather that defined my greatness. Instead, it was the profound realization that I had been great since the day I was born. God made me great; I was designed divinely and *with* greatness. My soul and my Being are great. I have, in fact, been great all my life the same way we are all great, created and conceived to be great in our own unique ways. Struggling to make it to the top of the mountain, on that dangerous and life-threatening edge of the road, I realized that greatness *is* within me and has been all along.

The struggles of that day revealed a profound truth: greatness is not something to be achieved but something we already possess within. We are encoded with it, given it, and it lives within the very essence of our being. Greatness is part of who we are, and the Great Maker gave us *all* greatness to be honed and utilized. I suddenly understood that all human beings are inherently great. We each have greatness, and we are made to be great in our own extraordinary way. Our job is to discover that greatness and then harness its treasured power. I found out that you truly reach greatness when you realize the greatness you seek you have already received.

The Greatness Factors

As you begin your journey on the road to *your* greatness, remember that your true greatness lies in how you live your life, treat others, and convey betterment in your environment. You do not have to climb a mountain to do this or put yourself in harm's way to discover it. You simply need to know that such greatness exists within you, and if you desire to tap into it, you will indeed find its magnificence.

It is also important to recognize that true greatness is not in grand gestures or wild rides; it resides in the daily choices you make. It's about how you live authentically, treat others with kindness and respect, and contribute positively using your innate gifts. You don't need to undertake extreme challenges or perilous adventures to access greatness. Instead, acknowledging and nurturing the inherent greatness that is already a part of you will bring about more greatness *through* you.

Each day presents opportunities to nurture and showcase your distinctive greatness. It is in the seemingly small efforts, minor actions, and heartfelt gestures that the fabric of greatness is woven. No matter how modest they seem, these everyday choices serve as the building blocks for something more endearing.

By embracing this perspective, you recognize that every interaction, decision, and contribution, no matter how modest, contributes to the tapestry of your greatness. Whether it's a kind word to a colleague, a moment of patience with a loved one, or a commitment to personal growth, each small act holds the potential for significant, lifelong impact. These cumulative efforts shape your journey and uplift those around you, sparking a chain reaction of positivity and improvement that expands far beyond just you.

Understanding that greatness is cultivated through consistent, purposeful actions allows you to focus on greatness's intrinsic characteristics. It encourages you to approach each day with intentionality and mindfulness, knowing that the accumulation of these small yet meaningful efforts will shape a kaleidoscope of lasting significance. As you continue to nurture and expand your unique greatness, you set the stage for meaningful transformations in your life and in the lives of others, creating a resounding legacy that will be remembered far beyond this present moment.

By embracing supportive values and enriching behaviors within your actions, you will uncover a profound sense of purpose and fulfillment. You will experience a richness that surpasses external recognition and connects with a greater part of yourself. Your actions are a testament to the transformative power of embracing your true self and living in alignment. Through this authentic expression of greatness, you will ensure greatness is catalyzed in you.

The I.G.N.I.T.E. Frequency

I often say, "The frequency we draw from influences the actions we take, which determines the impact we make." Think about that for a moment.

The energy you pull from, be it positive or negative, will directly influence the next steps you take, ultimately determining your results. Therefore, it is imperative to understand what frequency you are drawing from and what energy source you are connected to. In analyzing my own actions and results, I took the time to evaluate the source of influence to which I was connected to. *Did I listen to negative news and fill my mind with violent television? Or did I read empowering books, be around successful people, and appreciate the wonder of nature?*

I realized the sources I connected with significantly influenced how I lived and led my life. By reviewing those sources of influence, I decided to expose myself only to encouraging energies, beneficial frequencies, and uplifting vibrations. That shift filled my spirit, awakened my mind to profound opportunities, and enabled me to achieve great things. I then took it a step further and mapped out the frequency I wanted to surround myself with all the time. Using the essence of my brand, *Ignite*, I formulated a foundation of the frequency that would best serve me and ultimately assist others.

The I.G.N.I.T.E. Frequency is a power that I believe transcends mere words; it's a philosophy and vibration that can significantly influence your path to success. Each component of the I.G.N.I.T.E. Frequency is crucial in shaping your behavior and actions. They are the values you can tap into to provide a source of enduring passion.

The acronym I.G.N.I.T.E., which stands for Inspire, Give, Nurture, Improve, Transform, and Empower, represents key elements that support success. By integrating these principles into your daily routines, you create a positive framework that supports and enhances your future goals.

By embracing the I.G.N.I.T.E. Frequency, you tap into a powerful source that shapes your behavior and molds your outcomes. This enriching frequency helps you navigate life's challenges and opportunities with a clear sense of purpose and direction. Your actions align with your higher aspirations when you consistently draw from the values of *Inspire, Give, Nurture, Improve, Transform, and Empower*. This alignment not only propels you toward your greatness but also *amplifies the positive impact you have externally*. By consciously choosing to operate within the I.G.N.I.T.E. Frequency, you are setting a course for a life of *meaningful achievement and enduring greatness.*

Take a moment to connect with these key values and characteristics that will help deepen your connection to your greatness and fortify the excellence and enjoyment you seek.

- **Inspire** trust and respect through honesty, ethics, and consistency in actions and decisions. By embodying integrity, you light the way for others to follow, creating strong, meaningful relationships.

- **Give** your time, resources, and knowledge to others. Generous acts create a positive ripple effect, enhancing the well-being of your community and providing a sense of purpose and fulfillment.

- **Nurture** a more caring and connected community through empathy, kindness, and support. By uplifting those around you, you foster an environment of growth and mutual care.

- **Improve** through perseverance in the face of challenges. Resilient individuals inspire others to strive for progress, encouraging a mindset of strength and optimism.

- **Transform** your perspective by acknowledging your limitations and valuing others' contributions. This openness to learning and growth facilitates profound personal change.

- **Empower** through generosity; this involves sharing your strengths to help others gain confidence and control over their lives. Empowered individuals create empowered communities, driving collective success.

Integrating these elements into your daily life creates a beneficial foundation to propel you toward your goals. It's essential to recognize that having a set of guiding principles and ideals to navigate your journey toward greatness will get you there sooner and with measurable ease.

When you have a strong framework to draw from, especially one that is supportive and enriching, it fuels you to engage in even more positive and uplifting behaviors. This, in turn, creates even better and more beneficial outcomes. The frequency you draw from directly affects how you move forward, interpret interactions, and sustain your efforts. Each action, big or small, contributes to the end result. Therefore, utilize the highest vibration possible to activate and enrich the greatness within you.

I encourage you to use the I.G.N.I.T.E. Frequency in your life, but also to develop your own, customized frequency. Evaluate what frequencies match best with your intentions and then create a specific frequency calibration of the energy you want to cultivate. I find that when we take the time to analyze ourselves and produce tools that support our endeavors in an optimal way, we reach new heights and achieve unlimited greatness.

Your integrity inspires trust and respect, your generosity enriches your community, your compassion nurtures growth, your resilience drives progress, your humility transforms perspectives, and your empowerment fosters collective success.

Chapter 3

The Mindset of Greatness

The Power of Belief

I am sure you have heard it said before that *our beliefs determine our outcomes*. The stories we tell ourselves and the beliefs we hold on to can either propel us to greatness or keep us tethered to mediocrity. Just as Dumbo™ the Elephant's faith in holding a feather enabled him to fly, our belief systems empower us to achieve remarkable feats or hold us back from a life we never truly realize.

When Dumbo's mother told him the feather could help him soar, he faced a pivotal choice: to believe it was possible or to succumb to being *just* an elephant. He had to decide whether what he held true in his mind *would* make it happen or not. With faith, trust, and conviction, Dumbo gripped the feather and did indeed fly. He lifted himself off the ground and achieved his wish. The feather is not what made it possible; it was his belief in it that made it so.

A Modern Example of Belief

In contemporary history, a similar story of belief shaping reality can be seen in the journey of Paralympic athlete Amy Purdy. After losing both legs below the knee to bacterial meningitis, Purdy faced a future that seemed devoid of her dreams. However, she chose to believe in her ability to overcome her circumstances. With determination, she learned to walk, then snowboard, and eventually became a world-class Paralympic snowboarder. Despite her physical limitations, Purdy's belief in her potential allowed her to transform her reality and achieve greatness.[1]

Drawing from the transformative power of our mindset shapes our path to greatness. Our thoughts and beliefs can alchemize our potential and transform our inner fears into meaningful directions. By consciously choosing empowering thoughts, we can reshape our reality and unlock our greatness. This mental alchemy requires us to be vigilant about the quality of our thoughts and intentions in fostering a winning mindset.

Almost two decades ago, I coined the phrase 'negginym,' using it whenever my children said something negative or disempowering. I then added the phrase 'possinym' to train their brain to think of a more encouraging thought to counteract that negginym. Possinyms were much more powerful because they created an optimistic viewpoint overriding any limited form of negginym thinking. *I can't do that*, when possinymed becomes *Of course, I CAN do that. I'm not good enough* turned into *I am totally good enough. People don't like me; I'll never find my way; I can't make it*. All went from negginyms to possinyms by saying; People *do like me; I always find my way, and I know exactly what I must do to achieve that.* Shifting to possinym language and using positive statements prompts the mind into more supportive thinking and a winning belief system.

Having shared this philosophy with my customers, friends, and co-workers,

---

[1] https://www.paralympic.org/amy-purdy

possinyms have become a main staple in my training, and all my clients know me for asking them the vital question, "Can we possinym that?" They often chuckle but soon switch from negative thinking to positive, engaging, encouraging thoughts. As I have grown and evolved, possinyms have elevated into not just positive thinking but also into having an 'anything is possible' positive mindset. Possinyms remind us that *everything is thought*, and we can *choose to think* in the negative, or we can 'possinym it' and activate positive conviction and enriching results.

What has made possinyms and negginyms so prevalent is that we all need to *think* better and, therefore, *do* better. When I ask a person to think in terms of possinym, and they do so, they in turn, tell their brain to switch to a positive way to proceed. When we use a negginym, like *can't*, *shouldn't*, and *never*, we set the tone for failure right out of the gate. When we switch to possinyms, like *can*, *will*, and *absolutely*, we flip the switch and step into creating something greater. Then, we begin to see the possibilities and manifest the outcomes we desire.

Much like Dumbo believed he could fly by holding onto a feather, you, too, must decide whether you want greatness or not. This distinction is vital in forming the pathways and mindset that will bring your greatness forth. You get to choose; it is your decision. *Do you believe you are great and have yet to discover it, or do you feel you are the one person in all the world who missed getting the greatness that has been given to everyone else?*

If you've opted to believe in your greatness, bravo! By embracing this belief, you're aligning yourself with the possibility of achieving extraordinary things. On the other hand, if you feel like the one person who has been left out of having greatness, I'll happily tell you that this is your negginym mindset at work. Your old programming and conditioning may have led you to doubt that your greatness lies within. Your belief systems define 'your truth,' not the fact that you indeed have greatness in you, *without any doubt.* You are just at a place where you have yet to connect with it and see it for the greatness that it is.

Identifying Limiting Beliefs

Engaging in self-analysis is crucial to accessing your beliefs effectively. By looking inward and asking probing questions, we can unlock hidden assumptions or ideas that may be holding us back. Awareness of these beliefs gives us the power to shift or eliminate them. To access your beliefs effectively and unlock your potential for greatness, engaging in self-reflection is required. This process involves looking inward with curiosity and honesty and questioning the assumptions that shape your thoughts. By becoming aware of these views, you gain the insight needed to shift or eliminate those that no longer serve your highest aspirations.

Self-Analysis Exercise:

- **Create a Quiet Space:** Find a peaceful environment where you can introspect without distractions. This could be a comfortable corner of your home, a quiet park bench, or a serene spot in nature.

- **Set Aside Dedicated Time:** Allocate a specific period for reflection. This could be a few minutes each day or a longer session weekly, depending on your preference and schedule.

3. Questions to Explore:

- *What do I truly believe about my own capabilities and potential?*

- *Are there any beliefs I hold about success or failure that limit my efforts?*

- *How do I perceive challenges and setbacks? Are these perceptions possinyms or negginyms?*

- *What stories or narratives do I constantly tell myself about who I am and what I can achieve?*

- *Are there any beliefs I have inherited from past experiences or societal influences that no longer serve me?*

Write Down Your Insights: Writing down your thoughts and responses to these questions is a powerful way to deepen your self-analysis and foster personal growth. Here's how journaling can benefit you:

- **Clarity and Reflection:** Writing allows you to clarify your thoughts and gain deeper insights into your beliefs and perceptions. When you put pen to paper (or type on a screen), you engage both your logical and creative faculties, helping to articulate complex feelings and ideas.

- **Tracking Progress:** Keeping a record over time enables you to track your progress and evolution. As you revisit earlier entries, you may notice shifts in your thinking, new perspectives gained, or challenges overcome. This retrospective view can provide encouragement and motivation on your journey toward greatness.

- **Identifying Patterns:** By consistently documenting your reflections, you can identify recurring patterns or themes in your beliefs and behaviors. Recognizing these patterns empowers you to make informed decisions about which beliefs to reinforce and which to reshape.

- **Emotional Release and Healing:** Journaling can also serve as a form of emotional release. It allows you to express and process feelings of doubt, fear, or uncertainty, freeing up mental space for more constructive thoughts and actions.

By committing to regular reflection of the thoughts, beliefs, and opinions you have and those that can shift, you empower yourself to actively shape your mindset and emotions, paving the way for greater personal fulfillment and success. As you uncover limiting beliefs or outdated narratives, approach them with compassion and curiosity. Challenge each belief by asking yourself whether it aligns with your aspirations and potential for greatness. Replace limiting beliefs with affirmations and possinyms that empower and support your journey.

Engaging in such self-analysis exercises with openness and dedication can lead to profound shifts in your mindset. Remember, uncovering and transforming beliefs is a journey of self-discovery and growth. Embrace it as an effective tool on your path to uncovering your full potential.

Decide that the thoughts you entertain will only be those that propel you forward and create the life you dream of. Filter your thoughts to ensure they work in your favor, and choose to believe in the power within and the greatness you possess. Use your thoughts to mold your future and encourage your actions. Surround yourself with sources that inspire and motivate you toward greatness, for that is how greatness unfolds.

Chapter 4

The Alchemy of Thoughts

Visualization and Affirmations

On your journey toward greatness, your mind is your most powerful ally. Your thoughts and beliefs shape your reality, guiding your actions and influencing your outcomes. Two essential tools in the mindset arsenal are *visualization* and *affirmations*. These practices can transform your inner landscape, aligning your mindset with reaching new places and yet-to-be experiences. Visualization and affirmations can create a profound impact on our attitudes and activities. They are the added bonuses your mind needs to move from maybe to absolutely!

Having never cycled 10,000 kilometers before, I had to visualize myself cycling that distance, climbing those hills, and reaching the finishing line. I encouraged myself with positive affirmations that would help me when the muscles in my legs were hurting, or the callus on my hand was in pain. Every pedal I did across ten provinces was achievable only because I used *my mind to see it first and my thoughts to believe it was possible.*

Those same skills were used when I began my first business, wrote my first book, made my first sale, and followed my philanthropic endeavors to build my first school in a foreign country. Every big idea and *yet-to-be-experienced desire* had to first be formulated in my mind for it to birth into my reality. The power of visualization and affirmations had to be a cornerstone in helping turn my dreams into tangible attainments.

When I started my first business, I vividly imagined every detail—the office setup, the team members, the satisfied clients, and the moment when the business would break even and start making a profit. This clear mental picture kept me motivated through the initial struggles and uncertainties. Each day, I affirmed my capability and the business's success, reinforcing my belief in its viability. Visualization became my daily ritual, guiding my actions and decisions with unwavering confidence.

Writing my first book was another significant milestone that began with visualization. I saw myself holding the finished book, reading positive reviews, and speaking at book launches. Such mental imagery provided the inspiration and perseverance needed to overcome writer's block and the fear of rejection. I used affirmations to combat self-doubt, repeating statements like "I am a talented writer with a story that resonates with readers," "I can write wonderfully," and "People will enjoy my book!" These affirmations bolstered my confidence and commitment to the project, ultimately leading to its victorious completion.

One of my most fulfilling experiences has been my philanthropic work, particularly building my first school in Lombok, Indonesia. That monumental endeavor required not only a vision of the completed school but also a deep belief in its impact on the community. I visualized the children learning, playing, and growing in a safe and nurturing environment. Affirmations such as "I am a catalyst for positive change and literacy" kept me focused and driven despite the challenges and complexities of an international undertaking.

In all these endeavors, the common thread was the use of visualization and affirmations to shape my mindset and curate my actions. Every idea, ambitious goal, and yet-to-be-experienced desire had to be vividly imagined and firmly believed in my mind to see it to fruition. By cultivating a mental environment where success is seen and affirmed daily, *I could manifest my dreams into reality.*

The Power Behind Visualization

Visualization and affirmations are not just abstract concepts but practical tools that have guided me through each step of my journey. They have empowered me to navigate challenges, seize opportunities, and achieve milestones that once seemed distant or unattainable. Visualization is more than just daydreaming; it's a deliberate mental rehearsal of desired outcomes. When we visualize, we activate the same neural pathways as we do when we physically act. This mental practice helps to train the brain that is possible and capable and has already been done.

To succeed at cycling my 10,000-kilometer goal, I had to cycle between 100 and 150 kilometers daily. This was the first time I had cycled that much. Thirty to forty kilometers was my average, which was sporadic at best. As spring came late that year and snow was still falling in May, I was unable to cycle outside and practice any extended lengths. Instead, I spent my time indoors, visualizing every aspect of the road. I imagined my legs pumping the pedals and saw my hands on the handlebars. I envisioned the landscape before me: the long stretch of road and the rolling hills. I felt my heart pumping, my lungs breathing, and the satisfaction I would feel at the end of the day. The ride became real to me in my mind before I ever even mounted the bike.

The best part of the story is, on the very first day of our ride, having never been that far from my home or out on the open road, I was able to cycle 98 kilometers with ease and success. My body knew what to do because I had seen it in my mind repeatedly. Everything felt easy and possible because I had fully visualized it first.

The effects of visualization and affirmations are not just anecdotal but supported by numerous studies and expert opinions. For instance, Dr. Joe

Dispenza, a neuroscientist and author, emphasizes the power of visualization in his work.[2] He explains that "the brain doesn't know the difference between a real memory and an imagined one," meaning that vividly imagining an outcome can create the same neural pathways as actually experiencing it (Dispenza, 2019).

In sports, athletes frequently use visualization to enhance their performance. Michael Phelps, the most decorated Olympian of all time, is known for his rigorous visualization practice. Before every race, he mentally rehearsed the entire event, visualizing every stroke and turn. This practice helped him stay focused and prepared for any unexpected situations during the actual race (Hyman, 2016).[3]

Visualization and You

Visualization can be a key component in activating the greatness you want to achieve. The following explains why visualization is so powerful.

- **Clarify Goals:** Visualization helps you to define and crystalize your goals with precision. By picturing the end result vividly, you set a clear direction for your efforts and outcomes.

- **Boost Confidence:** Repeatedly visualizing success builds your confidence and self-belief. Seeing yourself succeed in your mind's eye reduces fear and anxiety, making you more assured in your abilities.

- **Enhance Performance:** By mentally rehearsing every detail, you prepare yourself for the real event, improving your skills and readiness.

---

[2] Dispenza, J. (2019). Becoming Supernatural: How Common People Are Doing the Uncommon. Hay House, Inc.
[3] Hyman, M. (2016). The Phelps Phenomenon. Sports Illustrated.

- **Motivate Action:** Visualization acts as a powerful motivator, encouraging you to take risks and push past your comfort zone.

- **Overcome Obstacles:** Visualizing positive outcomes helps you to anticipate and mentally prepare. This enables you to approach challenges with a problem-solving mindset.

To help you become competent at incorporating visualization into your daily practice, here are some actions you can easily and continuously do to integrate this technique into your greatness-building routine:

- **Morning Visualization Ritual:** Spend 5-10 minutes each morning visualizing your day ahead. Imagine yourself successfully completing your tasks, feeling confident and accomplished. See and feel the positive interactions with others and the satisfaction of achieving your goals. This sets a positive tone for the day and primes your mind for success.

- **Goal Achievement Visualization:** Choose a specific goal you want to achieve. Close your eyes and vividly picture every detail of accomplishing this goal. Imagine the process, the challenges you overcome, and the final triumphant moment. Engage all your senses— see the environment, hear the sounds, feel the emotions. Repeat this exercise daily to reinforce your commitment and motivation.

- **Relaxation and Stress Relief Visualization:** Find a quiet place and take a few deep breaths. Visualize a serene and peaceful scene, such as a beach, forest, or any place that makes you feel calm. Focus on the sights, sounds, and smells of this place. Let this mental image wash away your stress and fill you with tranquility. Use this exercise whenever you need a mental break or stress relief.

- **Performance Enhancement Visualization:** Before engaging in a specific task or activity, visualize yourself performing it perfectly. Whether it's a presentation, a sports activity, or a creative project, see yourself executing each step flawlessly and confidently. This exercise helps improve your actual performance by mentally rehearsing and preparing for success.

- **Future Self Visualization:** Spend time imagining your ideal future self. Visualize where you want to be in 5 or 10 years. Picture your surroundings, your accomplishments, and how you feel in that future. Consider the steps you need to take to get there and the qualities you must develop. This exercise not only motivates you but also provides a clear vision to strive toward, helping you align your daily actions with your long-term goals.

By consistently practicing visualization exercises, you'll strengthen your ability to use your mind to achieve your dreams and cultivate an even more cohesive roadmap to your greatness.

Practical Visualization Techniques

I like to say, "Nothing worth something is accomplished from nothing," meaning you must invest in it if you desire it. Simply thinking about visualizing won't yield results; you must take the time to visualize to reach the desired outcome actively. If you have never used visualization before to accentuate your greatness, here are some tips to get started:

- **Create a Clear Mental Image:** Start by closing your eyes and imagining your goal in vivid detail. Include all senses—sight, sound, smell, taste, and touch.

- **Use Guided Visualization:** There are many guided visualization audios and videos available that can help you focus your mind and enhance your practice.

- **Daily Practice:** Dedicate a few minutes each day to visualize your goals. Consistency is key to making visualization a powerful habit.

Visualization serves as a profound bridge between imagination and achievement, where the seeds of your dreams are nurtured into tangible realities. By cultivating a clear and detailed mental picture of your desired outcomes, you not only set a course for success but also Ignite the creative forces within you. In embracing visualization, you tap into a reservoir of potential that propels you forward with unwavering conviction. It is the art of seeing beyond present circumstances and into the realm of possibility, where every thought holds the power to shape your destiny.

What you focus on with intention and passion, you inevitably draw closer to manifestation and cultivate a deep sense of alignment between your inner aspirations and external actions. This alignment becomes the fertile ground where dreams take root and flourish into reality, guided by the unwavering belief in your ability to create and manifest greatness. Every visualization session becomes a sacred act of co-creation with the universe. Embrace this practice wholeheartedly, for it holds the key to unlocking the boundless greatness that awaits you on the path to realizing your dreams.

Chapter 5

The Power of Words

Words Carry Energy

Try this: put your hand up to your mouth and say "hate" or "bad." Feel the force of air accompanying these words, and recognize how it impacts your hand with a certain weight. Now, say "love" or "goodness" and notice how the energy feels lighter yet expansive as it flows outward into the Universe.

Similar to how a butterfly's gentle flap in the Amazon can set off a chain reaction leading to a hurricane in the Gulf of Mexico, words, too, possess this transformative power. Initially subtle, their energy grows with force and intention. Each word spoken is like a seed planted in the fertile soil of the cosmos, influencing the flow of reality.

Imagine your words as cosmic messengers, carrying vibrations that resonate far beyond immediate perception. They shape not only how others perceive you but also how you perceive yourself and your abilities. Consider the immense responsibility and potential: *if the Universe were to amplify and manifest everything you spoke about, wouldn't you want every word to be a catalyst for greatness and growth?*

I sometimes remind myself that every word I say is being broadcasted on a cosmic speaker, echoing through the vast expanse of the Universe. Each word carries with it a resonance, a vibration that reverberates far beyond my immediate surroundings. Like a symphony conductor, I have to know that I wield the power to orchestrate these vibrations, influencing the outcomes and dictating exactly the outcomes I desire. Using possinyms over negginyms, I am telling everything around me my true beliefs.

Consider the implications that every thought and every utterance shapes your reality, creating implications that extend beyond your awareness. The Universe listens intently to your words, interpreting them as intentions that shape your life's course. This vast amplification transforms every word you say into profound acts of creation.

With this awareness, speaking becomes an art form—an expression of your innermost desires and beliefs. Every word becomes saturated with purpose, infused with energy, and riddled with the power to create. What you speak aloud, you invite into existence, drawing nearer those aspirations and experiences that align with your words. Therefore, speak with mindfulness and clarity, for your words resonate not only within but also beyond. They ripple through the fabric of time and space, connecting you to the universal symphony of creation. Embrace the responsibility and opportunity to co-create with the Universe, ensuring that every word spoken contributes to the harmonious and prosperous life you want to lead.

Choose Your Words, Influence Your Greatness

Consciously choosing words and affirmations is a practice of aligning with the creative forces to conspire *with* you positively. Words channel the energy within and around us to cultivate a reality that reflects our highest aspirations. As you speak, visualize your intentions flowing outward, creating a benevolent tidal wave of greatness that attracts similar energies.

Affirmations are positive statements that reinforce our beliefs and shape our self-perception. Here are a few reasons why affirmations are so powerful. When repeated regularly, affirmations can:

- **Rewire the Brain:** Positive affirmations can create new neural pathways, replacing negative thought patterns with empowering beliefs.

- **Boost Self-Esteem:** Affirmations help build confidence and self-worth, making us more resilient in facing challenges.

- **Enhance Focus:** Repeating affirmations keeps our goals top of mind, helping us stay focused and aligned with our purpose.

Affirmations also have a strong foundation in psychological research. A study published in the journal *Social Cognitive and Affective Neuroscience* found that self-affirmations can activate the brain's reward centers, leading to increased feelings of self-worth and reduced stress (Cascio et al., 2016[4]). This neurological evidence supports the idea that repeating positive statements about oneself can lead to real, measurable changes in the brain.

In business, Oprah Winfrey, a renowned media mogul, has often spoken about the role of affirmations in her success.[5] She credits much of her achievements to her daily practice of affirmations, stating, "The words you speak become the house you live in" (Winfrey, 2015). By consistently affirming her goals and abilities, she created a mindset that allowed her to overcome obstacles and achieve unparalleled success. Affirmations, on the other hand, are positive statements that we repeat to ourselves to instill a mindset of success and positivity. They work by reprogramming your subconscious mind, replacing negative beliefs with empowering ones.

By recognizing the tactile impact of words and the profound analogy of the butterfly effect, we empower ourselves to speak with clarity, compassion, and purpose, making sure each word uttered is a deliberate step toward building a world where kindness, resilience, and greatness prevail.

---

[4] Cascio, C. N., O'Donnell, M. B., Tinney, F. J., Lieberman, M. D., Taylor, S. E., & Falk, E. B. (2016). Self-affirmation activates brain systems associated with self-related processing and reward and is reinforced by future orientation. Social Cognitive and Affective Neuroscience, 11(4), 621-629.
[5] Winfrey, O. (2015). What I Know For Sure. Flatiron Books.

As you incorporate affirmations into your daily lifestyle, you will begin magnifying what you see unfolding for yourself. Affirmations, when done consistently, produce the following results:

- **Reinforcing Beliefs:** Regularly repeating affirmations helps to reinforce positive beliefs about ourselves and our capabilities. This reinforcement gradually shifts our mindset, making us more resilient and optimistic.

- **Reducing Stress:** Affirmations can reduce stress and anxiety by focusing our thoughts on positive outcomes and possibilities. This shift in focus helps us to remain calm and composed, even in challenging situations.

- **Improving Mental Health:** By counteracting negative self-talk and limiting beliefs, affirmations contribute to better mental health and emotional well-being. They promote a positive self-image and a healthy sense of self-worth.

- **Encouraging Persistence:** Affirmations remind us of our goals and why we pursue them. This constant reminder keeps us persistent and determined, even when faced with setbacks or slow progress.

- **Creating a Positive Environment:** When we regularly use affirmations, we create a positive mental environment. This positivity attracts similar energies and influences, enhancing our overall experience and interactions.

The art of using affirmations lies in their strategic integration into our routines and thought patterns. Repeating affirmations regularly reinforces desired beliefs and goals, aligning our subconscious mind with our conscious deliverables. This practice enhances self-awareness and cultivates resilience and optimism in the face of challenges.

To incorporate affirmations effectively, choosing statements that resonate deeply with your goals and values is essential. These statements should be framed in the present tense, as if they are already true, to amplify their impact. For example, affirmations like "I am confident and capable in all that I do" or "Abundance flows effortlessly into my life" affirm positive qualities and outcomes, reinforcing a mindset of abundance and success.

Integrating affirmations into daily rituals—such as morning routines, meditation sessions, or even brief moments of reflection—ensures their consistent application. This repetition strengthens neural pathways associated with positive thinking, gradually transforming limiting beliefs into empowering ones. Over time, affirmations become ingrained in our psyche, influencing how we perceive ourselves and navigate the world.

Moreover, affirmations possess a unique ability to attune us to the frequency of our desires, aligning our thoughts and emotions with the outcomes we seek. They act as beacons of intention, drawing forth opportunities and experiences that mirror our affirmed beliefs. In essence, the art of using affirmations lies in their transformative potential to elevate consciousness and manifest desired realities. By embracing affirmations as sacred work, we harness the creative forces of the universe to co-create a life aligned with our highest visions.

Crafting Effective Affirmations

Crafting an effective affirmation is both an art and a science, requiring clarity and intentionality.

- **Be Specific**

- **Use Present Tense**

- **Be Positive**

Begin by identifying a specific area of your life where you want to see positive change or growth. Whether boosting confidence, attracting abundance, or fostering inner peace, the affirmation should address this goal concisely and affirmingly.

Start your affirmation with "I am" or "I have," anchoring it in the present tense to affirm that your desired state already exists. This immediate declaration sends a powerful message to your subconscious, reinforcing the belief that you already embody this reality.

Next, ensure that your affirmation is a possinym and uplifting, focusing on what you want to manifest rather than a negginym or what you wish to avoid. For instance, instead of saying, "I am not afraid of failure," possinym it as "I am confident and resilient in the face of challenges." This intentional reframing directs your energy toward empowerment and growth.

Make your affirmation specific and precise, avoiding vague statements that may dilute its impact. Define precisely what you intend to achieve or experience, using vivid language that resonates with your emotions and aspirations. Visualize how achieving this affirmation will positively impact your life, enhancing your motivation and commitment to its realization.

Lastly, infuse your affirmation with emotion and excitement. Repeat it with zest and zeal, feeling the truth and energy behind each word. The more you emotionally connect with your affirmation, the more effective it becomes in rewiring your subconscious beliefs and aligning your thoughts with your desired outcomes.

Crafting an effective affirmation is about the words you choose and the energy and intention you infuse into them. By consistently repeating and embodying your affirmation, you activate the universal forces that support manifestation, empowering yourself to create the life you envision.

Affirmation Exercise

- **Consistency:** Write down three affirmations related to your goals. Repeat them aloud every morning and night for 30 days.

- **Daily Repetition:** Choose a few affirmations and repeat them several times each day. Repetition is crucial for embedding these beliefs in your subconscious.

- **Mirror Work:** Stand in front of a mirror, look yourself in the eye, and repeat your affirmations. This can be a powerful way to build self-confidence and reinforce positive beliefs.

- **Write Them Down:** Write your affirmations in a journal or on sticky notes placed around your home or workspace. This visual reminder keeps them at the forefront of your mind.

By incorporating these exercises into your daily routine, you'll be well on your way to developing a mindset of greatness and achieving your dreams.

The final step is to couple visualization with affirmations together—positive statements that affirm your capabilities and desired outcomes—this helps reinforce the mental image with the verbal declaration of intention. Together, visualization and affirmations cultivate a unified mindset that aligns your thoughts, emotions, and actions with the manifestation and progress. This integrated approach harnesses the creative energies of the mind and the Universe, empowering you to confidently pursue and achieve your dreams.

Here are some ways to integrate these practices:

- **Visualize While Affirming:** As you repeat your affirmations, visualize the outcome you're affirming. This creates a powerful synergy between your words and mental images.

- **Morning and Evening Routine:** Start and end your day with a few minutes of visualization and affirmations. This sets a positive tone for the day and reinforces your goals before sleep.

- **Affirmation Visualization Board:** Create a vision board with images and words that represent your goals and affirmations. Spend a few minutes each day looking at your board and visualizing your success.

Visualization and affirmations are not just motivational tools; they are essential practices for cultivating a mindset of greatness. By consistently applying these techniques, you can transform your beliefs, align your actions, and ultimately realize your unified greatness. Remember, the journey to greatness begins in the mind. Harness the power of visualization and affirmations, and watch your life transform in extraordinary ways.

Chapter 6

We Create Our Results

Actions That Reflect Greatness

The ultimate destination on the roadmap to greatness is living a life of purpose and impact. When on purpose and aiming for impact over accolades, you begin to act differently; your work becomes not a chore but an extension of who you are and the imprint you want to leave behind. As purpose stands at the forefront, you are more focused on those actions that encourage and reflect you as the best version of yourself. What once felt mandatory may no longer be in focus, and what things were coveted may seem frivolous. Purpose inspires actions that empower the essence of greatness.

Actions taken with integrity are the building blocks of our character and the foundation upon which our results are built. Integrity is not merely adherence to moral principles but a commitment to aligning our actions with our values and convictions. It's about consistency between our words and deeds, our thoughts and beliefs intertwined with the actions we facilitate.

By acting with integrity, we cultivate a reputation for reliability and honorability. Each decision made in alignment with our values strengthens our sense of self-worth and reinforces our commitment to ethical conduct.

Integrity becomes a guiding principle that steers us towards decisions that uphold our moral compass and contribute positively to the world around us.

No one could ride my bike across Canada for me, just as no one could get up every morning at 4 AM to write this book or stay up into the wee hours of the night to make sure my business was running on point. My actions lead to my results. It was the actions I took, based on my thoughts and beliefs, that enabled me to uncover the greatness that was just beneath the surface and waiting to shine forth in me.

Knowing Your Greatness

Many people believe they can't achieve greatness—perhaps they think they're too old, lack the desire, or doubt their capabilities. However, the truth is that each of us deserves to live in our greatness. We all possess a treasure trove of gifts waiting to be embraced and shared with the world. The universe is abundant, overflowing with prosperity and opportunities just waiting to be bestowed upon us. The key lies in taking action to demonstrate our readiness for these opportunities.

When we take decisive steps toward our goals, we not only bring success closer but also shorten the distance to achievement. Each action we take aligns us more closely with our aspirations, bridging the gap between where we are and where we want to be. It's a testament to our commitment and determination to manifest the greatness that resides within us.

Greatness is not defined by age or circumstance—it's a state of being that emerges when we courageously pursue our dreams and embrace our inherent potential. As you step into your greatness and foster its existence, you begin to follow these important principles to ensure more greatness is developed in you.

- **Consistent Positive Actions:** Small, consistent actions often speak louder than overarching gestures. Acts of kindness, maintaining a genuine attitude, and being dependable in everyday situations contribute significantly to the emergence of greatness.

- **Building and Nurturing Relationships:** Investing in relationships with supportive and like-minded family, friends, and colleagues strengthens your social fabric and creates a support system that benefits your greatness evolution.

- **Serving Others:** Volunteering, mentoring, and supporting causes that benefit the greater good are powerful ways to embody greatness. Service to others enriches your life and brings to the forefront what truly matters.

- **Lifelong Learning and Growth:** Great individuals are committed to continuous self-improvement. They seek out new knowledge, skills, and experiences, always striving to become better versions of themselves.

- **Leading by Example:** True leaders inspire others through their actions. By modeling the values and behaviors of greatness, they motivate and encourage those around them to follow suit.

Great leaders throughout history have consistently demonstrated these principles in shaping a better world. Their actions have left a lasting legacy of progress and positive change. Environmental stewards mitigate environmental degradation. Social justice leaders galvanized movements for equality and human rights; innovation and technological advancements have been driven by leaders who envision a future where technology serves humanity's collective good. Leadership in philanthropy and humanitarian aid has provided lifelines to communities affected by conflict, natural disasters, and poverty. These examples illustrate that greatness in decisive action and intentional behaviors has an unwavering impact on society.

I share this because greatness is interwoven with servant leadership. Greatness finds its noblest expression in the art of servant leadership, where leaders prioritize the needs of others above their own. At its core, servant leadership fosters an environment of trust and collaboration, where leaders empower the people they know to excel and innovate. Servant leaders lead by example, demonstrating integrity and ethical decision-making in every facet of their leadership. They prioritize the well-being of their families, ensuring that personal goals align with principles of fairness and social responsibility.

As stewards of greatness, we must embrace servant leadership that encourages a long-term perspective, where individuals invest in their development and growth. In essence, greatness in servant leadership lies in the transformative impact on individuals and communities. Through selfless dedication and a genuine desire to serve others, servant leaders inspire a shared vision of a better future where compassion and collaboration pave the way for sustainable growth and prosperity. Servant leadership thus becomes a cornerstone of greatness and a purpose we all can be proud to obtain.

Chapter 7

On The Road, Let's Go!

The Power of Intention

Setting clear intentions is the next step in igniting your greatness. Intentions are the north star that keeps you focused on your goals, helping you navigate the inevitable challenges along the way. I always emphasize the importance of clarity and purpose when training and mentoring. When your intentions are aligned with your true desires, you create a powerful force that propels you in a way that nothing can hold you back.

Let's take a moment to write down your intentions for all facets of your life—personal, family, health, and dreams. Be specific and bold. Instead of saying, "I want to be successful," articulate your intention clearly: "I intend to build a thriving business that empowers others." Clarity in your intentions is like fuel for your mind; it propels you forward and anchors you when the path ahead seems daunting.

Set intentions that align with your values and aspirations in your personal life. Whether it's fostering deeper connections with loved ones, pursuing hobbies that bring you joy, or cultivating a mindset of gratitude and resilience, articulate these intentions clearly. For example, "I intend to prioritize quality time with my family each week to nurture our connection."

When it comes to health, be proactive in setting intentions that support your well-being and vitality. Instead of vague goals like "losing weight" or "getting fit," set a clear intention such as, "I *will* cultivate habits that promote my physical health," and include regular exercise, balanced nutrition, and mindfulness practices.

Consider intentions that contribute to a harmonious and supportive environment in your family life. This could involve commitments to open communication, mutual respect, and shared activities that strengthen familial ties. For instance, "I intend to create a loving and supportive home environment where each family member feels valued and heard." Imagine the change and shift this will bring to creating a greater family.

Regarding your dreams and aspirations, dare to be bold in setting intentions that reflect your deepest desires and hopes for the future. Whether it's pursuing a career change, starting a passion project, or traveling to places you've always dreamed of, articulate these intentions with conviction. "I intend to manifest my dream of [specific goal or dream] by taking consistent and focused action toward its realization."

By writing down your intentions with clarity and specificity, you amplify your goals and program your mind and spirit to obtain them. This intentional focus helps you stay committed and on target, even during unprecedented times. Embrace the power of intention-setting as a "must-do" to shape your personal acceleration, enrich your relationships, enhance your well-being, and manifest your big dreams into your new reality.

Take a moment to write down your intentions. Be specific and visionary. Clarity in your intentions, along with boldness, fuels the journey and helps you stay committed even when the path gets tough.

Take the First Step

The journey to greatness begins with a single step. It might be as simple as enrolling in a course, reaching out to a mentor, or dedicating time each day to work on your passion project. The key is to take action, no matter how small it may seem. Each step you take is a testament to your commitment to igniting your potential.

Empower Others

Once you've embarked on your journey, the next step is to leverage your progress and experiences to empower others. This can be achieved through various means, such as sharing your knowledge and insights with those around you, mentoring individuals who are starting their own paths, or actively participating in community initiatives that promote growth and development. Remember, greatness is about personal achievement and uplifting and empowering those around you to reach their full potential.

Embrace Change

Change is pivotal on the path to igniting your greatness. It involves shedding old patterns and beliefs that no longer serve your growth and seeing change as a catalyst for transformation rather than something to fear. Cultivate resilience and adaptability to navigate challenges, viewing setbacks as opportunities for learning and growth. Keep your intentions clear and nurture the potential within you to guide you through tough times.

Build a Support System

No journey to greatness is solitary; building a supportive community is essential. Surround yourself with like-minded individuals who believe in your vision and encourage your progress. Seek mentors, peers, and friends who provide guidance, encouragement, and accountability. Engage with communities that align with your goals, participate in events, and connect with inspiring individuals to amplify your efforts.

Implement Self-Care

Self-care plays a crucial role in sustaining your journey. Prioritize your physical, emotional, and mental well-being through regular exercise, healthy eating, mindfulness practices, and adequate rest. I emphasizes a holistic approach to self-care, recognizing its role in replenishing your energy, enhancing creativity, and fortifying resilience. Make self-care a non-negotiable part of your routine to elevate your ability to realize your potential.

Celebrate Milestones

Celebrate your milestones along the way, regardless of their size. Acknowledge your achievements to honor your progress and reinforce your dedication to your goals. Reflection on your growth and lessons learned is vital. By sharing your successes, you celebrate your journey and inspire others to pursue their paths of possibility.

Give First and Give All You Can

At its core, this principle encourages a mindset of abundance rather than scarcity. It recognizes that by giving generously—whether it's time, expertise, resources, or emotional support—we contribute to a collective well-being that enriches both the giver and the receiver. Giving first signifies a proactive approach to building meaningful connections and fostering a spirit of reciprocity within communities.

Giving all you can involves wholeheartedly investing your energy and commitment to causes or endeavors that align with your values and aspirations. This could mean dedicating yourself fully to a charitable initiative, advocating for social justice, or mentoring individuals to help them unlock their potential. By giving all you can, you exemplify integrity and dedication, inspiring others to follow your lead and contribute their talents and resources toward shared goals.

These actions—taking the first step, empowering others, embracing change as a catalyst for growth, building a supportive community, prioritizing self-care, and celebrating milestones—are the DNA of greatness. They form the foundation upon which personal transformation and achievement thrive. Embracing change with resilience and adaptability, nurturing a supportive network, and prioritizing holistic self-care are essential steps on the journey to igniting one's potential. By celebrating every milestone, regardless of size, and sharing successes to inspire others, individuals honor their progress and contribute to a legacy of possibility. These actions empower you to reach your greatest potential, foster a life you will always be proud of, and exemplify the essence of true personal greatness.

The journey to greatness is ongoing. It is a continuous process of growth, learning, and transformation. I encourage embracing this journey with an open heart and a curious mind. The everlasting flame within you is a source of endless potential, capable of igniting your path and the paths of others. As you navigate your roadmap to greatness, hold onto the belief that you are capable of extraordinary things. Trust in the power of your inner knowing and let it guide you to a life of purpose, impact, and fulfillment. Always know that you have exceptional greatness in you.

Chapter 8

Your Unique Roadmap

Create Your Road Map

The roadmap to your greatness is a journey that begins with you!

By embracing the Ignite mindset, using words and visualization, setting clear intentions, and taking consistent action, you can forge a wondrous path just waiting to be discovered. Remember, your greatness lies within you, waiting to be unleashed and actualized. You now have the roadmap to get there and the process to enjoy every step of the way. Now, it's time to synthesize those insights into your personalized roadmap to greatness.

Use this chapter as a blank canvas and a master document to review often and fine-tune your goals and destinations. Let this summary be the vehicle you need to work at redefining your greatness often and finding the nuances that elevate you. Allow this to be your guidepost and map out your plan. Greatness is not a destination; it is a state of being and a way of life.

Enjoy mapping out your greatness, and I hope to see you along the road to achieve all that you dream of in your heart and in reality.

Clarify Your Vision

Reflect on your journey so far and distill your aspirations into a clear vision. *What does greatness mean to you?* Define your goals and intentions with clarity and specificity. Use affirmative language to articulate what you aim to achieve and why it matters deeply to you.

Identify Your Core Values

Consider the values that drive you—the principles that guide your decisions and actions. Align your goals with these core values to ensure your pursuit of greatness is meaningful and authentic. Your values will serve as your compass, keeping you grounded and focused amidst challenges and opportunities.

Visualize Your Intention

See exactly what you desire and take the time to write it out, draw it with colored pens, make a vision board, fill your home with visual quotes and references, and surround yourself with what shows your mind that it is already happening.

Design Your Strategy

Develop a strategic plan outlining the steps and resources required to achieve each goal. Consider the skills you need to develop, the networks you need to leverage, and the actions you need to prioritize. Identify potential obstacles and devise contingency plans to navigate setbacks effectively.

Cultivate Resilience and Adaptability

Acknowledge that your journey to greatness may not always be smooth. Embrace setbacks as opportunities for growth and learning. Cultivate resilience by maintaining a positive mindset, seeking support from your community, and staying adaptable in the face of change.

Nurture Your Support System

Surround yourself with individuals who believe in your potential and support your aspirations. Cultivate relationships with mentors, peers, and friends who inspire and challenge you. Collaborate with like-minded individuals who share your values and vision for mutual encouragement and accountability.

Commit to Self-Care

Prioritize your well-being throughout your journey. Incorporate self-care practices that nourish your physical, emotional, and mental health. Dedicate time for relaxation, reflection, and rejuvenation to sustain your energy and creativity.

Measure Progress and Celebrate Success

Regularly assess your progress toward your goals. Celebrate milestones—both big and small—to acknowledge your achievements and renew your motivation. Reflect on lessons learned and adjust your roadmap as needed to stay aligned with your evolving vision of greatness.

Inspire and Pay It Forward

As you progress on your journey, inspire others by sharing your experiences and insights. Pay forward the support and guidance you've received by mentoring others and contributing to your community. Your journey to greatness is not just about personal achievement but also about uplifting those around you.

Only use Positive Words

Finally, embrace the journey itself with curiosity, passion, and gratitude. Every step you take towards your goals, fueled by your vision and guided by your values, contributes to your growth and impact. Trust in your potential to use meaningful words to cultivate greatness in all aspects of your life.

By crafting your personalized roadmap to greatness, anchored in these principles and actions, you empower yourself to live authentically and purposefully. Your journey is unique, and each decision you make contributes to the legacy of greatness you're destined to create. Embrace the process, stay committed to your vision, and remember that you have everything within you to achieve extraordinary things.

Chapter 9

Living Your Genius

Loving Your Gifts and Talents

Greatness is not a destination but a journey, a continuous process of discovering and embodying the unique gifts that reside within each of us. While many tools and strategies can support our journey toward greatness, the most profound factor influencing our greatness is engaging in what we love, what we naturally excel at, and what fills our hearts with joy. This chapter will guide you to recognize and cultivate your "zone of genius"— the core of your innate abilities and passions. By living in this center, you can unlock what is truly great about you and live a purpose-driven life.

Every person on the planet has talents and skills. If the Great Maker gave the pelican a huge beak to scoop up fish while in flight, the giraffe a long neck to reach the highest branches, and a forest ant the ability to carry 40 times its size, then we can be sure that you too received a talent like no other. When we look around, we see endless examples of those who have tuned into their talent and found ways to utilize them. We have witnessed a child with the skills to play the violin with sublime precision, a man capable of jumping so high he can dunk a basketball in a towering hoop, a woman whose songwriting skills can bring people to tears of happiness. We all have glorious talents and gifts that, when we foster and cultivate them, become our greatest allies.

Identifying Your Zone of Genius

You may not have taken the time to awaken to what talents lie within you. Due to past conditioning, circumstances, pressure from others, or expectations from authority figures, you may be living life doing what you are supposed to but not what you are a genius at. We are all geniuses in our own way, and each one of us has a genius gift within us. Our job is to recognize our zone of genius and expand upon it. Real greatness is when we find that gift and share it lovingly with others in a way that enriches the world and brings about more happiness.

Take the time to establish just what is unique and precious in you by doing the following:

- **Reflect on Your Strengths:** List the activities and tasks that come effortlessly to you. *What do you do well without much effort? What have others consistently praised you for?*

- **Recall Your Joyful Moments:** Think about the times when you felt most alive and fulfilled. *What were you doing? Who were you with? What aspects of those experiences brought you joy?*

- **Seek Reflection:** Sometimes, others can see our strengths more clearly than we can. Ask friends, family, and colleagues what they believe your greatest strengths are. Look for patterns in their responses.

The Power of Passion

If no one has ever shared with you, passion is, in fact, the lifeblood of greatness. It is the driving force that propels us to pursue our dreams with fervor and determination. When we are passionate about what we do, we are naturally motivated to put in the time, effort, and dedication required to excel. Passion ignites a fire within us, making the journey toward greatness not just doable but exhilarating. It transforms difficult tasks into meaningful endeavors and challenges into opportunities for growth. Passion fuels creativity and innovation, allowing us to push beyond our limits and achieve extraordinary results. When our work resonates deeply with our hearts, we are more resilient in the face of setbacks and more committed to our goals. Passion makes us more alive, engaged, and capable of tapping into our full potential. It is the essence that accentuates our greatness, turning our innate talents into powerful forces of impact and fulfillment.

Discovering Your Passions

When you are passionate about what you are doing, you are more likely to put in the effort and perseverance required to excel. Passion energizes you, making the journey enjoyable and the challenges manageable. It is a powerful motivator that keeps you focused and committed.

Use the following exercises to help fuel the passion that will propel you toward greatness.

- **Explore New Activities:** Try out different activities and hobbies. Pay attention to how you feel while engaging in them. *Which activities light you up and make you lose track of time?*

- **Reflect on Your Interests:** Consider the topics and issues you are naturally drawn to. *What do you love reading about, discussing, or learning? What subjects can you talk about endlessly?*

- **Connect with Your Inner Child:** Think back to your childhood dreams and interests. *What did you love doing as a child?* Often, our early passions hold clues to our true calling.

Embracing Your Innate Talents

Many people undervalue their natural talents because they seem easy or commonplace. However, what comes easily to you may be a significant challenge for others. Recognizing and embracing your innate talents is crucial to living from the center of your genius. These talents are gifts meant to be shared with the world, and they hold the potential to make a significant impact.

Try doing the following and see what you discover:

- **List Your Achievements:** Write down your accomplishments, both big and small. *What skills and abilities did you use to achieve these successes?*

- **Identify Patterns:** Look for patterns in your achievements. *What common skills or talents were involved?* These patterns can reveal your core strengths.

- **Celebrate Your Gifts:** Acknowledge and celebrate your talents. Give yourself credit for the things you do well and recognize their value.

True greatness emerges at the intersection of passion and talent. When you engage in activities that you are both passionate about and talented in, you create a powerful synergy that leads to exceptional performance and fulfillment. This intersection is your zone of genius, where you can make the most significant impact.

Honoring Your Heart's Desires

Greatness is most prevalent in the lives of those who honor their heart's desires. It is not about meeting external expectations or following imposed paths but about listening to your inner voice and pursuing what truly matters to you. When you follow your heart, you align with your true self, leading to greater happiness and contentment.

When I was cycling across Canada, the plan was to finish at Cape Spear, the farthest eastern point in the northern hemisphere. Yet, when I arrived there, nothing felt like the dream I had envisioned. I wanted to cycle along the shoreline, up a hill, and to the foot of a glorious lighthouse indicative of the area. I wanted to get off my bike and walk to the very edge of the cliff and look over the vast sea that stretched beyond the horizon. I imagined a picture-perfect, emotional, and surreal moment encompassing the seventy-nine days I spent pedaling.

When I arrived at Cape Spear, it was none of these things. The road was amidst trees, and there was no ocean shore. The lighthouse was short and stumpy, there was a chained fence that prohibited access to the shoreline, and there was an entrance fee. Nothing about that moment filled my heart or made me happy, and none of it spoke to me in the way I had envisioned my accomplishment.

Immediately, I told my husband that this was not it, this was not the end of our ride or the spot that would mark my epic achievement. I used my phone and began searching for lighthouses in Newfoundland to find a picture of the perfect lighthouse on the shoreline of a cliff overlooking the ocean. When I found the perfect one, tall and majestic, overlooking the world, I told my husband we were going there!

I know it will be hard to believe, but the name of the town where that lighthouse stood was called Heart's Content! I promise you it is true! My husband and I cycled 230 more kilometers to make it to Heart's Content so I could cycle along the beautiful coastline, up a glorious hill, right to the foot of a red and white painted lighthouse on the very edge of a blustery but captivating cliff. I rode my bike to the very top and then got off and walked to the hillside, looking out all the way to England! I heard the sea birds cheering, the waves clapping, and my heart beating with the most joy and happiness. My heart was full and overflowing because I listened to it. I didn't do what was easy or practical. I did what made me happy and what would fill me with the *knowing* that I had indeed found the greatest moment while honoring my heart's desires.

That moment has been one of the greatest moments in my life, combining the success of reaching the finish with following my heart's inner happiness and listening to what mattered most to me, feeling the excitement and perfection of a dream coming true.

Listening to Your Heart's Desire

In all matters, I urge you to follow your heart's desire. Listen to the passion and purpose that lives with you from a heart place; not an ego or greed place, but a place of pure honoring yourself and doing what *lights you up*. When you align your actions with the deepest longings of your heart, you tap into an endless source of motivation and joy. This alignment brings a sense of fulfillment that transcends any external measure of success. Trust that your heart knows the way and that by following it, you will create a life that is not only successful but deeply meaningful and rich with contentment. Your heart's desires are the truest compass guiding you toward your greatest potential, leading you to a life of profound impact and authentic happiness.

I encourage you to do the following and connect with what your heart truly wants.

- **Quiet Your Mind:** Find a quiet place where you can sit comfortably and close your eyes. Take a few deep breaths and allow your mind to settle.

- **Ask Yourself:** *What do I truly desire?* Allow your heart to answer without judgment or analysis. Write down whatever comes to mind.

- **Reflect and Act:** Reflect on your heart's desires and consider how you can incorporate them into your life. *What steps can you take to honor these desires and move closer to your true calling?*

The Role of Exploration and Reflection

Exploration and reflection are vital in discovering your intrinsic skills and passions. Through exploration, you expose yourself to new experiences and possibilities, broadening your horizons and uncovering hidden talents. Reflection allows you to process these experiences, gaining insights into what resonates with you and what does not.

A mindset of greatness involves believing in your potential and embracing the journey of self-discovery and growth. It requires a commitment to nurturing your talents and passions and a willingness to step outside your comfort zone. By cultivating this mindset, you empower yourself to live from the center of your genius zone.

Greatness is like a muscle we need to strengthen and cultivate. Just like any muscle in our body, if ignored, it will weaken and atrophy. Consistent effort, dedication, and intentional practice are required to develop and maintain our inherent greatness. This means continuously challenging ourselves, seeking growth opportunities, and embracing the journey of self-improvement. By regularly engaging in activities that push our limits and expand our abilities, we not only preserve but enhance our unique talents and gifts. Remember, greatness is not a static trait but a dynamic quality that flourishes with mindful attention and persistent effort.

- **Try New Things:** Make a conscious effort to try new activities and experiences. Keep an open mind and embrace the unknown.

- **Journal Your Experiences:** After each new experience, take time to journal about it. *What did you enjoy? What felt challenging? What did you learn about yourself?*

- **Regular Reflection:** Set aside regular time for reflection. Review your journal entries and look for patterns and insights. Use these reflections to guide your future explorations.

- **Affirm Your Potential:** Create positive affirmations that reinforce your belief in your potential. Repeat these affirmations daily to build confidence and resilience.

- **Set Intentions:** Set clear intentions for what you want to achieve. Focus on your goals and visualize yourself succeeding.

- **Embrace Challenges:** View challenges as opportunities for growth. When faced with difficulties, remind yourself that they are stepping stones on your path to greatness.

By following these exercises and reflections, you will enhance your self-discovery and growth, uncovering the greatness that lies within you. In doing so, you will not only achieve greatness but also honor your heart's desires.

By taking the time to discover your zone of genius and honoring what fills your heart with joy, you can unlock a life of fulfillment and impact. Remember, the greatest factor in achieving greatness is doing what you love and shining brightly in *your* unique way.

Chapter 10

The Essence of Contentment

The New Currency of Success: Contentment

*I*n a world driven by constant striving, yearning, and an *insatiable desire for more*, true greatness is often misdirected. Many people equate success with the accumulation of wealth, accolades, or status. However, the new currency of success is not measured by external achievements but by deep, abiding feelings of contentment. Contentment is the number one marker of true greatness—not complacency, but a profound sense of fulfillment and peace.

Contentment arises when we align our lives with our true selves, living from the center of our genius and engaging in activities that fill our hearts with joy. It is the state of being satisfied with who we are, what we have, and where we are in our journey. Contentment does not imply a lack of ambition or growth; rather, it signifies a balanced pursuit of our goals, rooted in self-awareness and gratitude.

My friend Sarah always dreamed of making a difference in the lives of children. Despite societal pressure to pursue a more lucrative career from her parents, she followed her passion for teaching. Sarah always shares with me that she finds immense joy in seeing her students learn and grow. Her contentment is evident in her cheerful demeanor, the strong bonds she forms with her students, and the satisfaction she feels at the end of each day. Sarah's contentment stems from *knowing she is living her purpose and positively impacting the world.*

I recently met a man in San Francisco who had a talent for woodworking. He chose to turn his passion into a way to connect with people and enhance his creativity. He collects driftwood from the beach and pine cones from the forest and marries them together into stunning tiny sculptures He is passionate about the shapes that he carves, and the homes his creations end up in with the people he so graciously meets. He found fulfillment in his craft. Each piece he created was a testament to his skill and love for his work. His contentment was visible in his meticulous work, his pride in his creations, and the joy he felt when my husband and I bought a piece to bring home that reflected the two of us.

Signs of a Content Person

If you are longing to combine your greatness with your contentment, here are several key characteristics that distinguish deep contentment and greatness:

- **Gratitude:** Be a person who regularly expresses gratitude for what you have and the people in your life. Focus on appreciating the present rather than yearning for the future or pinning for yesterday.

- **Inner Peace:** Radiate a sense of calm and inner peace. Do not be easily swayed by external circumstances and maintain a balanced perspective.

- **Fulfillment:** Engaged in activities that bring you joy and fulfillment. Find work and hobbies that align with your passions and talents.

- **Positive Relationships:** Forge strong, meaningful relationships. Invest time and energy into nurturing meaningful connections with others.

- **Purpose-Driven:** Have a clear sense of purpose and direction. Ensure your actions are guided by your values and intrinsic motivations.

- **Self-Acceptance:** Accept yourself and embrace both your strengths and weaknesses. Do not compare yourself to others but celebrate the unique journey that you are on.

Cultivate Contentment

In the pursuit of greatness, contentment is the ultimate measure of success. It is not about accumulating more but about finding joy and fulfillment in who you are and what you do. By living from the center of your genius, embracing your innate talents and passions, and honoring your heart's desires, you can achieve true greatness. Let contentment be your guide, and you will find that the most profound sense of success comes from within.

To cultivate contentment, it is essential to shift our focus from external achievements to internal fulfillment. This involves:

- **Self-Reflection:** Regularly reflect on your values, passions, and talents. Align your actions with your true self.

- **Thankfulness Practices:** Develop a habit of being thankful at all times. Appreciate the small joys and blessings in your daily life.

- **Mindfulness:** Practice mindfulness to stay present and grounded. Let go of unnecessary worries about the past or future.

- **Purposeful Living:** Engage in activities that resonate with your core values and passions. Seek fulfillment in your everyday actions.

Through the exercises and practices shared here, you are taking the vital steps needed to identify and cultivate the unique gifts and talents that reside within you. Remember, greatness is not an elusive destination but a continuous process of growth, expansion, and self-actualization. The simple act of seeking your greatness is the first and most important step toward finding it.

Progress on your journey comes from consistent effort and the courage to put one foot in front of the other. Be patient with yourself and celebrate each and every step along the way. Understand that greatness does not arrive overnight; it is the result of sustained effort, care, and dedication. Every small victory and moment of self-awareness contributes to the development of your greatness. Embrace the process with a tender heart and a resilient spirit, knowing that each step, no matter how small, is a testament to your commitment and perseverance.

Nurturing your greatness is akin to tending a precious seed. It requires the essential ingredients of self-love, self-care, and self-acceptance. Just as a seed needs water, sunlight, and nourishment to grow, your journey to greatness needs daily attention and intentionality. Treat yourself with kindness, acknowledge your progress, and give yourself the grace to grow at your own pace. By providing these nurturing elements, you create an environment where your greatness can flourish and thrive. Trust in the process, and know that through your dedicated efforts, you are destined to uncover and embody the greatness that lies within you.

"Contentment is not the fulfillment of what you want,
but the realization of how much you already have."
– Anonymous

Chapter 11

Greatness & Breakthrough

Discover Your Breakthrough

Embarking on the journey to find your greatness often begins with welcoming a transformative breakthrough. This initial step is crucial, as it involves breaking free from the limitations and barriers that have been holding you back. Without overcoming these obstacles, it's challenging to reach your full potential and make a significant impact.

In working on your breakthrough, you may find yourself delving into the process of identifying personal and professional obstacles that may be hindering your progress. These could range from self-doubt and fear of failure to external challenges such as lack of resources or support. Understanding these obstacles is the first step toward addressing them effectively.

Breakthrough work means exploring practical strategies to facilitate mindset shifts, resilience-building techniques, and the invaluable benefits of overcoming limiting beliefs. By taking the time to facilitate a breakthrough, you overcome the setbacks and reframe your thinking to support solutions and possibilities where there once was none. Breakthrough awakens the mind to what is possible and what the mind can *perceive it can achieve.*

Identifying Your Obstacles

To facilitate a breakthrough try incorporating these steps into your process.

- **Reflect on Past Experiences**: Look back at past experiences to uncover patterns or events that may have contributed to current challenges. Journaling and introspection can be effective tools in this process.

- **Self-Assessment Tools**: Utilize self-assessment tools and frameworks to identify specific areas for improvement. Personality tests, SWOT (Strengths, Weaknesses, Opportunities, and Threats) analysis, and feedback from peers can provide valuable insights.

- **Set Clear Goals**: Establishing clear, actionable goals can help you focus on overcoming specific obstacles. Break down these goals into manageable steps to track your progress.

Strategies for Breakthroughs

It is essential to equip ourselves with effective strategies that pave the way for breakthroughs. Effective strategies provide you with practical tools and actionable insights to overcome obstacles and unlock your true greatness. These strategies, carefully curated and shared throughout our exploration, offer a roadmap to navigate the challenges and uncertainties you may face. By implementing those techniques, you can transform setbacks into stepping stones and propel yourself toward achieving your personal and professional goals. Remember, breakthroughs are not accidental; they are the result of deliberate actions and a mindset committed to growth and excellence.

Here is a reminder of what you have already learned and what strategies you need to implement to awaken one's inner greatness.

- **Embrace a Growth Mindset**: Adopting a growth mindset involves believing in your ability to learn and grow. This mindset shift can empower you to tackle challenges with confidence.

- **Develop Resilience**: Building resilience involves learning to adapt and bounce back from setbacks. Techniques such as mindfulness, stress management, and positive thinking can enhance your resilience.

- **Seek Feedback and Mentorship**: Constructive feedback and guidance from mentors can accelerate your progress. Mentors provide valuable perspectives and support that can help you navigate challenges.

Benefits of Breaking Through

Experiencing a breakthrough is a transformative moment that can significantly impact your personal and professional life. Breakthroughs foster a deep sense of accomplishment and self-confidence. When you overcome a significant challenge or achieve a long-sought goal, you prove to yourself that you are capable of more than you previously thought possible. This newfound confidence can inspire you to tackle even greater challenges and pursue your dreams with renewed vigor. Breakthroughs often lead to increased creativity and innovation. As you push past obstacles, you are forced to think outside the box and develop new strategies and solutions. This creative problem-solving not only helps you overcome the immediate challenge but also equips you with valuable skills that can be applied to future endeavors.

Breaking through also enhances your resilience and adaptability. By navigating difficulties and emerging victorious, you build mental and emotional strength. This resilience enables you to handle future setbacks with greater ease and to view challenges as opportunities for growth rather than insurmountable obstacles.

Breakthroughs can also significantly improve your relationships and network. As you achieve your goals and demonstrate your capabilities, you attract like-minded individuals who are also striving for excellence. These connections can provide support, inspiration, and valuable opportunities for collaboration.

The process of breaking through can lead to a deeper understanding of yourself and your true potential. As you stretch your limits and explore new territories, you gain insights into your strengths, passions, and purpose. You also gain:

- **Clarity and Focus**: Achieving a breakthrough provides clarity on your goals and the steps needed to achieve them. This focus can lead to more effective decision-making and strategic planning.

- **New Opportunities**: Overcoming obstacles can open up new opportunities for personal and professional growth. You may discover new skills, passions, or career paths.

- **Personal Fulfillment**: The sense of accomplishment from achieving a breakthrough can lead to increased confidence and fulfillment. This positive momentum can propel you towards your legacy goals.

"As a mentor and legacy builder, my mission is to empower and guide individuals toward achieving breakthroughs that unlock their true potential. I wholeheartedly believe that transcending our limitations is pivotal to realizing greatness. Through dedicated effort, I work diligently with my clients to identify and overcome the barriers holding them back. My approach focuses on shifting negative thought patterns to ones that foster positivity and possibility. Together, we cultivate a mindset that embraces challenges as opportunities for growth and transformation. By nurturing this mindset and encouraging resilience, I help my clients navigate their journey toward achieving the success and fulfillment they deserve."

Join the Ignite Your Breakthrough Program

If you are wanting to facilitate your own breakthrough and step into a new awakening of just how great you are, I invite you to join *Ignite Your Breakthrough*; a transformative mastermind I teach each week that focuses on building your mental mindset that enriches your greatness. By identifying and overcoming obstacles, embracing a growth mindset, and seeking to understand your gifts, you can unlock your full potential and set a strong foundation for your greatness journey. Giving you new found clarity, focus, and inner resilience, you become well-equipped to achieve your dreams and make a lasting impact. We all need support and guidance at different times in our lives. If you feel you are ready for this, classes take place each week, sign up here or click to find out more, otherwise email support@igniteyou.life, or book a discovery call with me to discuss it in more detail at calendly.com/jbtime.

Chapter 12

Words of Greatness

There is Greatness Within us All

Our journey toward greatness is always woven within the threads of our unique stories—the tales of how we found our greatness, lost sight of it, and rediscovered it again. These narratives are not just personal accounts but powerful lessons that shape our understanding of ourselves and our place in society. Sharing our poignant stories is not only cathartic but also transformative, for ourselves and those who hear them.

Having published over 750 personal transformational stories, I have witnessed firsthand the profound impact of storytelling. I firmly believe that when you tell your story, you not only transform your own life but also touch the lives of many others. Stories have a remarkable ability to transcend barriers, fostering compassion, closeness, and empathy among us. They awaken our hearts, illuminating the greatness within ourselves and others.

Encouraging others to share their stories of dedication, overcoming challenges, and celebrating victories is a passion of mine. Through the process of writing and reflecting on their experiences, individuals tap into a deeper sense of their worth and value in the world. Writing becomes a powerful vehicle for self-exploration, self-awareness, and personal growth.

I find immense joy in guiding people through this process, witnessing their exploration of self-awareness and the profound shifts that occur when they share their stories. By offering their narratives with the intention to inspire or help others facing similar challenges, individuals often experience a shift in consciousness. They gain new insights and perspectives that empower them to embrace their greatness more fully and authentically.

In essence, storytelling is not just about recounting events; it is a journey of self-discovery and empowerment. It connects us on a human level, reminding us of our shared experiences and collective resilience. As we share our stories of triumph and transformation, we create a stage of inspiration that encourages others to embark on their own journeys of self-discovery and greatness.

If you've ever felt the desire to share your story or write a book about the journey you've been on, I am here to support you wholeheartedly. Your story holds immense power—it may be exactly what another person needs to read to ignite their own journey towards their greatness. I have seen how personal stories serve as catalysts for transformation and inspiration. Your experiences, challenges, and triumphs have shaped you into the person you are today, and by sharing them authentically, you have the potential to profoundly impact others who are navigating similar paths.

Why Share Your Story?

Writing your story for yourself could be instrumental in expanding your greatness. Firstly, it promotes deep self-reflection and clarity, allowing you to understand your journey, identify strengths, and learn valuable lessons. Secondly, it serves as a powerful tool for personal empowerment and healing, enabling you to validate your experiences and find closure with past challenges. Most importantly, sharing your story inspires and connects with readers, offering them insights, encouragement, and a sense of solidarity in their own struggles. Your narrative has the potential to uplift others, showing them that transformation and greatness are achievable through resilience and self-discovery.

- **Self-Reflection and Clarity:** Gain deep insight into your journey, identify strengths, and learn valuable lessons.

- **Empowerment and Healing:** Validate your experiences, find closure with past challenges, and promote personal growth.

- **Inspiration and Connection:** Inspire and connect with readers, offering insights, encouragement, and solidarity in their own journeys of transformation and greatness.

- **Create Lasting Impact**: Your story has the power to inspire, educate, and transform lives. By sharing your story and insights, you can create a lasting impact on readers and contribute to their growth and development.

If you desire to write your story, I invite you to join one of our empowerment compilation books. In this transformative four-month program, you will embark on a journey of self-discovery, collaboration, and publication alongside a group of like-minded individuals. Together, we will uncover the depths of your unique experiences, craft your narrative with care and authenticity, and ultimately publish it to inspire others.

Throughout the program, you will receive guidance and support to articulate your story effectively, ensuring that your voice shines through authentically. This process is not just about writing; it's about embracing your journey, finding clarity in your experiences, and empowering yourself through storytelling. By participating in this empowering journey, you will not only contribute to a powerful compilation of stories but also connect with a community of individuals dedicated to personal growth and transformation.

I have had the blessing to have printed over 24 compilation books at the time of this book's printing. They have been in many areas and themes, including, parenting, health & wellness, purpose, courage, faith, forgiveness, entrepreneurship and many more. I guarantee if you look to see what book we are doing next, it will be exactly the right book for you. Go to our website. www.igniteyou.life and look under upcoming books to apply.

If you prefer to write a full solo book, then I invite you to join the *Ignite Your Solo Book* program, where I will guide you through the entire process of conceptualizing, writing, publishing, and marketing your book. This weekly program helps you to explore the reasons why writing a book is a crucial step for embracing your greatness and thriving. I provide a detailed roadmap to help you navigate each phase of the book-writing process, from choosing a compelling topic to finalizing the manuscript. Additionally, we will discuss effective strategies for publishing and marketing your book to ensure it reaches and resonates with your target audience. Throughout this program, you will have a clear understanding of the steps involved in writing your story and the immense value it brings to your legacy. You will be equipped with the knowledge and tools to embark on your book-writing journey and create a lasting impact through your words.

Join the Ignite Your Solo Book Program

Ignite Your Solo Book is a powerful way to share your legacy with the world. By connecting with other authors in this immersive program, you can create a compelling and impactful book that enhances your authority, reaches a wider audience, and leaves a lasting legacy. With the right guidance and support, you can bring your book to life and make a meaningful contribution to your greatness and the lives of those around you. Classes take place each week, sign up here or click to find out more, otherwise email support@ igniteyou.life, or book a discovery call at calendly.com/jbtime.

Chapter 13

Sharing Your Greatness

Ignite Your Signature Talk

Remember how I shared in Chapter 5 about the power of our words? Well, your words contain greatness within them. In fact, my good friend and the number one motivational speaker on the planet, Les Brown, has built his entire career on speaking about greatness. If you search for him on Google™ or YouTube™, you will hear his profound voice speaking on greatness, saying, "YOU HAVE GREATNESS IN YOU!" I love hearing Les share these words. He even uses them on his answering machine, and sometimes I call him just to listen to his message and hear his empowering reminder. His sentiment is powerful and touches me to my core. During a breakthrough moment, at one of the lowest points in my life, I heard Les speak this phrase, and it changed the trajectory of my life forever. He reminded me of the greatness I had lost and instilled in me a desire to rediscover it.

As you know words have the power to heal, transform and uplift. Sharing words through public speaking is one of the most effective ways to thrive within your greatness and share greatness to those that need to hear it. A well-crafted and delivered signature talk can captivate and inspire, leaving a lasting impression on your listeners and like Les did for me, change a person's life and remind them of their intrinsic greatness.

I now teach people how to create their powerful message and share their innate greatness in a class called *Ignite Your Signature Talk*. It is designed to help you develop and deliver a powerful presentation that showcases your expertise and greatness. This award-winning program will support you through the process of crafting your talk, perfecting your delivery, and promoting your message to reach more people. This enjoyable program offers strategies for building online platforms, seeking speaking opportunities, and collaborating with organizations to maximize both theirs and your greatness.

Join Ignite Your Signature Talk

Ignite Your Signature Talk is a powerful way to share your message with the world. By crafting a compelling message, delivering it with confidence, and promoting it effectively, you can captivate and inspire your audience. With the right preparation and strategies, you can use public speaking to make a lasting impact and achieve GREATNESS. This program also has a certification and the ability to be part of the *Ignite Speaker Bureau*. Classes take place each week, sign up here or click to find out more, otherwise email support@ igniteyou.life, or book a discovery call at calendly.com/jbtime.

Unleash Your Greatness

In Chapter 6, we explored the concept of creating greatness through the steps we take in life. Reflecting on my own journey, I realize that each step has been instrumental in shaping who I am today. Looking back, I see not just the challenges and triumphs but also the lessons learned and the growth experienced along the way. It is this perspective that has inspired me to create a transformative program called "Ignite Your Legacy."

Life is a series of steps, each one leading us closer to our aspirations and dreams. As I embarked on my own path, I encountered obstacles that tested my resolve and moments of clarity that illuminated my purpose. Through these experiences, I discovered the power of resilience, determination, and the unwavering belief in the possibility of greatness.

That inspired me to create a program called: *Ignite Your Legacy.* It is more than just a program; it is a journey of self-discovery and empowerment that enables you to build an empire that will support you and the dreams you have to help others and make a difference. It is designed to guide individuals through their personal and professional evolution, drawing from my own experiences and insights gained over years of dedication, growth and uncovering what I consider *my* greatness.

The ultimate goal of "Ignite Your Legacy" is to empower individuals to create a lasting impact in their lives and the lives of others. By honing their strengths, cultivating resilience, and aligning their actions with their values, participants embark on a journey of personal excellence and fulfillment. Whether through career advancements, personal achievements, or community contributions, the program equips individuals with the tools to leave a meaningful legacy.

The *Ignite Your Legacy* program stands out because it integrates four powerful programs into one comprehensive approach to greatness building. By focusing on *breakthroughs, book writing, branding,* and *public speaking,* this program provides a holistic and strategic path to creating a lasting impact. It includes the unique benefits of each of the four Ignite programs and illustrates how they collectively contribute to building a legacy.

Traversing your journey to achieve greatness requires a multifaceted approach that encompasses personal growth, knowledge sharing, brand development, and effective communication.That is why in a desire to go beyond what others are doing I have offered what no one else in the self-development world is conquering; four programs per week. To truly *Ignite Your Legacy*, you must be willing to take bold action and step outside your comfort zone. This means working on your personal development, enhancing your skills, building your business, and shaping your unique philosophies with the world.

The Ignite Your Legacy Mentoring Program

Each program within the *Ignite Your Legacy* mentoring program addresses a crucial aspect of tapping into your greatness, ensuring you have the tools and support needed to achieve your goals. From overcoming obstacles to establishing your authority and sharing your vision with the world, these programs provide a comprehensive framework for success. If you are drawn to this idea and feel ready to make legacy a destination on your roadmap, let me help you and be the mentor you require. If building your legacy is something you aspire for to ensure your greatness reaches millions, let's connect. Book a discovery call with me directly at calendly.com/jbtime and let's discover the next phase of sharing your greatness.

Chapter 14

Beginning Your Road to Greatness

As we reach the end of this journey together, I want to take a moment to express my heartfelt gratitude for allowing me to be a part of your quest for greatness. Writing *The Roadmap to Greatness* has been an incredible experience, and I am deeply honored that you chose to embark on this transformative journey to finding the greatness that lies within you.

Throughout these pages, you have explored the profound concept of greatness—not as a distant destination, but as a continuous journey of self-discovery and self-actualization. You have delved into the importance of recognizing and nurturing your innate talents, passions, and zone of genius. You have learned that true greatness is not about meeting external expectations or societal standards, but about embracing what makes you uniquely you and living from the center of your being.

As you move forward, I encourage you to cherish the lessons and insights you've gained. Remember that greatness is not a static state but a dynamic process that evolves with each step you take. Continue to explore, reflect, and cultivate the gifts that reside within you. Trust in your abilities, follow your heart's desires, and honor what fills your soul with joy and contentment.

Your greatness is a beacon that not only illuminates your path but also inspires and uplifts those around you. By living authentically and passionately, you contribute to a world where true success is measured by the deep, abiding feelings of fulfillment and contentment. Remember that each day offers a new opportunity to make a lasting impact. Your greatness is achieved through the choices you make, the kindness you extend, and the passion you pursue. Embrace the journey with courage and conviction, knowing that your efforts today will inspire future generations.

As you move forward, remember that your greatness is a living, evolving testament to who you are and what you stand for. Continue to dream big, act boldly, and lead with your heart. Surround yourself with those who inspire you, challenge you, and support you on this journey. Together, you can create a ripple effect of positive change that extends far beyond your immediate reach.

Let this book serve as both a guide and a source of inspiration as you continue to actualize your greatness. Your journey is just beginning, and the world is waiting for the unique impact only you can make. Go forth with confidence, knowing that you have the power to become great. Here's to your ongoing adventure and the extraordinary pathway to greatness you are destined to create.

Thank you for allowing me to guide you on this journey. May you continue to discover and embrace the greatness that lies within you, and may your life be filled with purpose, joy, and boundless possibilities. The open road is just waiting for you... you now have the most powerful roadmap you need to live in the center of your magnificent greatness. Have fun, and let the world see just how great you are.

The greatest feeling is discovering the greatness that exists within.
~ Lady JB Owen

Author Biography

Lady JB Owen is a fearless female leader, 25-time bestselling author, global publisher, international brand builder, award-winning businesswoman, celebrated humanitarian, coveted speaker, trainer, legacy mentor, and knighted lady. JB's entrepreneurial spirit and dedication to making a positive impact have led her to combine business with inspiration in an innovative way. Forbes Magazine has dubbed JB the "Heart-Centered Publisher," Entrepreneur Magazine has called her a "Female Entrepreneur Determined to Change the World," and Apple News added her name to their "Top 50 Entrepreneurs to Watch." She combines purpose, passion, and possibilities in everything she does on her mission to Ignite every life on the planet and create a ripple effect of change.

As founder and CEO of Ignite Publishing™, the leader in Empowerment Publishing. Lady JB has published over 800 authors from 47 countries, going international best-sellers in 13 countries in 197 categories. Her goal is to inspire others through Ignite Moments™, those moments that inspired them to empower others. As a publisher, she teaches individuals how to tell their stories in a way that transforms their lives and empowers them to create the lives they envision for themselves and others. As a legacy Mentor, she mentors on giving back, raising the consciousness, and creating lasting impact for future generations. Lady JB believes we all can ignite our lives, the lives of others, and humanity.

Lady JB is also the CEO of JBO Global™, which produces award-winning, eco-friendly products. She is an Executive Producer at Ignite Moments Media™ and is devoted to the betterment of others through the power of uplifting one another.

In recognition of her profound humanitarian and entrepreneurial efforts, Lady JB was knighted by the Royal Order of St. Constantine the Great and St. Helen in 2022. Her humanitarian work spans building a school in impoverished areas, spearheading the Ignite Humanity global movement, and establishing the Ignite Humanity Foundation Fund. In her relentless pursuit to raise literacy awareness, she has cycled thousands of kilometers for charity, including a journey to Alaska, across Canada, and to Mexico with her husband on their tandem bike. Her humanitarian work was further honored in 2022 when she was bestowed with the Ignite Humanitarian Award at the *Be Great!* Foundation.

Lady JB Owen combines purpose, passion, and possibilities in everything she does on her mission to Ignite every life on the planet and create a ripple effect of change. She believes that when we come together in unity and harmony with the desire to raise the consciousness of all humanity, magic will happen.

She is the mother of two children and two stepchildren and lives in Canada with her husband, Peter. She travels extensively, has new adventures, and reminds everyone that *anything and everything is possible*.

Contact Lady JB Owen

http://calendly.com/jbtime

info@igniteyou.life

Websites

www.jbowen.website

Socials

FB: Lady JB Owen

IG: Lady JB Owen

LinkedIn: Lady JB Owen

Contact Ignite

support@igniteyou.life

Websites

www.igniteyou.life

www.ignitehumanity.life

Programs

courses.igniteinstitute.life/igniteyourlegacy

courses.igniteinstitute.life/breakthrough

courses.igniteinstitute.life/billionairebrand

courses.igniteinstitute.life/solobookclub

courses.igniteinstitute.life/innercircle

https://market.igniteyou.life/join-ignite-inspires

Socials

FB: Ignite Humanity Community

Ignite You

Ignite Possibilities

Ignite Moments

IG: Ignite You

Charity Initiatives

ignitehumanity.life/donate

Free Ebook

https://forgiveness.igniteyou.life/ebook

https://market.igniteyou.life/writingprompts

Free Meditation

https://affirmations.thepinkbillionaire.com

Free TV Episodes

https://watch.ignitehumanity.life/

Book recommendations:

Awaken Giants by Tony Robbins

Think and Grow Rich by Napoleon Hill

E-Myth by Michael E. Gerber

The 10X Rule by Grant Cardone

The Greatest Salesman in the World by Og Mandino

The Science of Getting Rich by Wallace D. Wattles

Good to Great by James C. Collins

Big Magic by Elizabeth Gilbert

What makes me GREAT!

_____

_____

_____

_____

_____

_____

_____

_____

_____

_____

_____

_____

_____

_____

_____

_____

_____

_____

_____

_____

_____

What I believe about my GREATNESS

Ways I can develop my GREATNESS

_____

_____

_____

_____

_____

_____

_____

_____

_____

_____

_____

_____

_____

_____

_____

_____

_____

_____

_____

_____

_____

_____

_____

_____

What being GREAT means to me

www.ingramcontent.com/pod-product-compliance
Lightning Source LLC
Chambersburg PA
CBHW051226120626
46547CB00013B/1530